A N…
Term…
and The…

A Methodology for Term Papers and Theses

Paul Haffner

Gracewing.

First published in 1996

Gracewing
Fowler Wright Books
2 Southern Ave, Leominster
Herefordshire HR6 0QF

ISBN 0 85244 381 1

Typesetting by
Action Typesetting Ltd, Gloucester, GL1 1SP

Printed by Cromwell Press
Broughton Gifford, Wiltshire, SN12 8PH

Table of Contents

Introduction

This little book is a short guide to essential methodology for writing papers and theses in the Roman ecclesiastical faculties and universities. It is not exhaustive, but simply furnishes the main elements of a method which should help the student to make a consistent series of references and a coherent bibliography as well as producing a scientifically respectable text. It could also prove useful to authors of academic books.

The manual is based on my own experience in writing a doctoral dissertation as well as other books and papers. It takes into account my experience in marking various pieces of written work, where I have been able to see the main pitfalls and problems which the student encounters. The method provided here is congruent with that used in documents of the Pope and the Congregations of the Roman Curia, as well as with those approaches employed in various pontifical universities. It should also be useful elsewhere *mutatis mutandis*, and in subjects other than philosophy and theology. This work regards method as a means rather than as an end and so the student should be able to see the wood for the trees. It does not 'legislate' on details of typography or page layout, since more and more students are using computers, in which a word-processing package arranges automatically what previously had to be thought out with a typewriter. It is my hope that the student would be able to adapt it where necessary to his or her particular needs. The choice of a methodology allows freedom, for any consistent method is acceptable. However, this choice is not arbitrary, since some forms of methodology lend themselves more easily to a logical application. It is to be hoped that the present volume contains a straightforward and logical approach.

This book owes much to Tom Longford and Jo Ashworth whose generous help brought it to birth.

Rome, 1 May 1996
Feast of St. Joseph the Worker

Chapter 1

The Art of Study

'These studies are an impetus to youth, and a delight to age; they are an adornment to good fortune, refuge and relief in trouble; they enrich private life and do not hamper public life; they are with us by night, they are with us on long journeys, they are with us in the depths of the country.'

Cicero, *Pro Archia*

'Patience too is to have its practical results so that you will become fully-developed, complete, with nothing missing.'

Letter of St. James 1:4

1.1 Sources

Writing papers, articles or theses involves the know-how of consulting various types of sources. This forms the raw material from which the final product is shaped, so great care should be exercised in excavating the various mines of information.

1.1.1 Libraries

Normally the required books and periodicals will be found

in university libraries, but sometimes it may be necessary to approach a more specialized collection. Readers can save themselves time by learning the system which is used to catalogue the books and periodicals. The older method was a system of index cards arranged according to author and/or title of book or periodical. Each book or periodical is numbered, and the library is organized according to these numbers. Now most library cataloguing systems are being updated with computers. In the event of any particular difficulty, a librarian should be approached.

1.1.2 Archives

Here an archivist will find the required material, so he or she should be furnished with a clear idea of the date and content of what is being sought after. Archives are often organized according to the position number, which relates to the topic of the material, and the protocol number which determines the particular document you are dealing with. The protocol number usually consists of a figure and a date. For example 3626/84 is the three thousand six hundred and twenty-sixth document classified in the year 1984. Elsewhere, the serial number of the manuscript (MS 40) and the folio number (f.26) are used. These are not the only methods for arranging archives, so the researcher should try and understand a little of the system of any archive that he or she consults. The relevant parameters should be taken down, as they will be required for citation in the references. Also, it may be necessary to consult the material another time, if something is missed on the first attempt. It will greatly help the archivist if the researcher can quote the parameters of the required document. Permission should be sought from the archivist in order that the material consulted may be quoted in a text, especially if this is to be published, for archive material may be confidential.

1.1.3 Interviews

Interviews and questionnaires should not be used unless absolutely necessary, for academic written work is different from journalism. Conducting a survey and analyzing the results constitutes an advanced series of scientific skills which may prove very time consuming. In a piece of philosophical or theological written work, the primary sources would rarely be the results of a survey. It may be better to consult the results of a survey which has already been processed and analyzed. However if this type of source is employed, the purpose of the interview should be made clear to the interviewee and his or her written permission should be obtained to quote the results in the write-up. The interviewee should be carefully recorded on tape (or other medium). It would also be correct, once the first draft of the work has been written, to ask the interviewee to see if he or she is satisfied with the way they have been quoted and to verify that their thought has not been distorted. This verification process may be difficult or even impossible if there are a very large number of people interviewed. It will be necessary to state in the written work whether the material gathered during interviews was recorded on video-tape, audio-tape, or simply written down. This material should be kept, as it may be needed later to defend what has been written.

1.2 The use of computers

> 'Mysterious machines are the exclusive products of science-fiction writers.'
>
> Stanley Jaki, *Brain, Mind and Computers*

1.2.1 Basic rules

It is wise never to spend too long at one session working with a computer as this can tire the eyes. The correct bodily posture should also be maintained when working at a video-terminal.

Work carried out on a computer should always be saved regularly, so that if there is a power cut, and there is no protective device on the system, a large quantity of material will not be lost. Programs (like *WordStar*) which automatically make a back-up copy of each document are always preferable.

A backup floppy disk should be kept of all the work done, and this backup disk must always be updated by saving onto it the new work completed by the end of a morning or afternoon of writing. In this way, if material on the first disk or the hard disk becomes corrupted, the risk of losing precious hours of work will be avoided. It is also wise to keep a printout (hard copy) of the work as it proceeds.

If the work is written with a word-processing package on a computer, much of what would need to be done on a typewriter is automatically carried out by the program itself. Within a chosen standard paper size (such as A4) the computer program has a set left and right margin, a set top and bottom margin, a set page length (often around 25 lines per double-spaced A4 page). The program also arranges where the page numbers are placed and performs more complex functions such as the organization of footnotes and end notes. It is important to make the most of the program to obtain from it the final page layout that is desired. In general, it is better to utilize a simple software package which is suitable for the particular needs which the researcher encounters in the job at hand, rather than a system which is highly sophisticated, but which will be more trouble than it is worth.

Hardware and software should be matched. In other words, the word-processing package should be matched with the particular printer that is connected to the computer. Otherwise various characters may come out in a strange way, or else the page length may not be right. Also, it is sometimes necessary to experiment with page length and margins so that the page is printed as it appears on the screen or at least as desired! Matching is also necessary to obtain the kind of print or typeface that is required. Most word-processing packages come supplied with several print fonts.

It should be ensured that the disk drive(s) of the computer are cleaned occasionally, so that any build up of dust or foreign matter is avoided. Only cleaning products especially sold for computers should be employed. An anti-virus system should be employed to check that no unwanted guests are present in the system! Diskettes should never be accepted from unknown sources.

1.2.2 Practical points

Widows and orphans should be avoided as far as possible. An *orphan* occurs when the first line of a paragraph appears alone at the bottom of a page. It also happens when a title or subtitle within a piece of written work is placed right at the bottom of a page and then the text to which it refers is on the next page. In other words, the title is orphaned from its text. The title should be moved onto the next page to stand along with its text.

A *widow* occurs when the last few words of a paragraph lie alone at the top of a page, so that these words are widowed from their sentence. These few words should be put on the previous page, or else, if this is not possible, the whole sentence should be placed on the next page.

A check should be made to ensure that the computer program makes correctly hyphenated line-breaks for the language employed in the piece of written work. A problem can arise in this respect if an Italian or Spanish word-processing package is being used, but the written work is in English.

Care should be taken that the right margin of the page is 'justified' for papers and theses. A justified text has all lines the same length so that its edge is straight. A 'ragged' right edge is acceptable for a letter, but not in academic written work. Similarly it should be ensured that a line doesn't begin with punctuation, which should have appeared at the end of the previous line. This happens when a space has been left between the last letter of a sentence and the punctuation mark; in this case, the justification mechanism of the computer program can throw the punctuation mark down to the next line.

It may seem elementary, but care should be taken to see that the pages of any piece of written work are numbered. Many computer programs have a device for omitting page numbering. So it is worthwhile to check that page numbers and all other necessary elements are present in the written work by having a look at the page preview system which allows the writer to view the pages as they will actually appear when they are printed; most recent computer programs are endowed with this type of system.

It is wise to keep up-to-date on information technology as far as finances permit. With the electronic transmission of data and scanning techniques, it is already possible to import written passages from the sources into the written work, avoiding the need for keying-in large blocks of text. This could be a great time saver.

1.3 Scientific Research

In scientific research, the first principle is intellectual honesty, the second organization, the third clarity.

1.3.1

By intellectual honesty, is meant that in any written text, ideas found elsewhere are always acknowledged, stating their precise source. It would be seriously wrong to present as one's own idea what belongs in the work of some other author. Research aims to seek 'the truth, the whole truth and nothing but the truth' and so all the dimensions of truth must be scrupulously respected.

1.3.2

As regards organization, it is useful to make index or note cards for collecting material. Index cards are either of the traditional, mechanical kind consisting of a series of cardboard slips which are kept in a box in alphabetical order of authors or of subjects, or else are of the electronic variety. The latter involves a computer program in which each index 'card' is a page on a screen which then forms part of a data-base sorted and stored on disk. The following method is a useful one for collecting material from books, articles and manuscripts:

a) The whole text should not be copied, but rather notes are taken of the basic ideas or the expressions which are striking.
b) It is unwise to put too many ideas on one card, because then it may not be easy to find the ideas again, and research will become complicated with the risk of not being able to find information when it is needed at the writing stage. At the same time, *all* the necessary information should be written down at an early stage. Much time is wasted on data lost through carelessness. It is frustrating to half-remember something which has been seen, but not copied down. Direct quotes should always be distinguished by placing them within inverted commas.
c) A careful distinction should be made between page numbers, folio numbers, column numbers, and article numbers. Pages are numbered on both sides (abbreviated to p. in the singular and pp. in the plural) and are most often found in books and journals. Folios are numbered only on the front side (abbreviated to f. in the singular and ff. in the plural) and are often found in archive material. Columns are often found in patristic tomes and are numbered continuously, normally at the top of blocks into which the work is divided typographically. The abbreviation for a column is c. in the singular and cc. in the plural. Article numbers, often encountered in medieval tomes, are found in the margins alongside the division of the book in this fashion. The abbreviation is a. in the singular and aa. in the plural.
d) It is essential to write on the index card, at the head of the notes and the copied text, all the bibliographical information, namely: the surname and initials of the author(s), the date published, the place published

(which is normally a city), and the publishing house. Similarly, with an article from a journal, it is necessary to copy all the necessary data, namely: the name of the journal, the volume number, and the year. Care should be taken to find out whether the pages in successive issues of the journal are numbered continuously or whether the numbering starts again with each issue. In the latter case, it is necessary to copy down the issue number (within a given year) as well as the volume number in order to specify completely where a given passage is to be found. The relevant page numbers must be copied down. If great care is exercised at this stage, much time will be saved later at the writing stage of the essay or thesis.

Example: This index card summarizes an entire book

P. Haffner, *Creation and Scientific Creativity: A Study in the Thought of S.L. Jaki* (Front Royal, Virginia: Christendom Press, 1991)

This work aims to be 'an introduction to Father Jaki's vast researches and profound insights on the close ties between the exact sciences and the Christian theology of Creation' (p.8). After a brief Introduction, Chapter 1 sketches a portrait of Stanley Jaki, showing that although the latter began his work in ecclesiology he has become a world-famous authority on cultural, philosophical and theological questions relating science and religion. Recognition has come to him, above all, in the form of the Templeton Prize (1987) and honorary membership of the Pontifical Academy of Sciences (1990). Chapter 2 shows how Jaki approaches science in its phenomenology and essential incompleteness; it then shows how Jaki considers the metaphysical-epistemological basis of science (p.29). Jaki's phenomenology of science underlines its pitfalls and prospects (Chapter 3); the unique rise of science in the high Middle Ages is offset against its stillbirths in all ancient cultures. This unique viable birth points to a realist metaphysics, which in turn has as its matrix the Christian doctrine of creation. Jaki's treatment of this Christian doctrine of creation as enunciated in Scripture and Tradition is examined in Chapter 4; the bond between the Christian notion of Creation and the dogma of the Incarnation is stressed. Further, 'the connection between Creation and Incarnation has a direct impact on Christian anthropology' (p.64). Chapter 5 deals with the adequate view of man in the Christian philosophico-theological vision, and shows how Jaki rejects materialistic and idealistic conceptions of the human person, including those flowing from Darwinism, from considerations of artificial intelligence or from wrong-headed views of extra-terrestrial intelligence.

The last three chapters of the book constitute an evaluation of Jaki's thought on the themes dealt with in the first part. Chapter 6 discusses how Jaki's critics view his discoveries concerning history and modern science; Chapter 7 then notes the crucial thrust of Jaki's thought in terms of the realist perspective which allows us to arrive at the cosmos as 'the totality of consistently and most specifically interacting entities, a totality of contingent but rationally coherent and ordered beings' (p.48 cf. p.105). The section on Christology and cosmos makes clear what is specifically *Christian* in Jaki's notion of Creation. The final chapter traces the capital importance of Jaki's thought for the Church's pastoral mission today, given his creative conformity with her Magisterium; his close correlation with the teaching of Pope John Paul II is illustrated. The book ends where it began with a statement of the first article of the Creed. Each chapter is headed by an appropriate aphorism; there are extensive notes (pp.133–172) and an exhaustive bibliography (pp.173–200).

1.3.3

Clarity is important to specify the purpose of the research undertaken and to know what is being sought out and where it is to be found. As a piece of written work progresses, material may well be found which will alter somewhat the direction of the work. This should not be a cause for concern; it is quite normal for research to be shaped by what is found in the course of study. Economy is one of the fundamental principles required in order to achieve clarity. Any superfluous material should be avoided, whether this be in the method, in the text or in the notes.

Chapter 2

The Essay

'I am convinced more and more day by day that fine writing is next to fine doing.'

John Keats, *Letter to J. H. Reynolds*

2.1 Basic ideas

Many rules for writing a seminar paper also apply to a term paper, an elaboratum or an article for a journal. A seminar provides training in two basic scientific skills. One is how to present a scientific paper at a conference or congress, the second is how to prepare a paper for publication in a learned journal, or in the acts or proceedings of a congress. The same fundamental methodological skills are employed here as will later be applied in writing a thesis or even an academic textbook.

A seminar paper, normally 10–15 pages long with double-spacing, is a work of synthesis which constitutes a proof of the ability to introduce a theme and develop it to its logical conclusions. Thus, it is helpful to make an outline plan before beginning to write the text. It is also an exercise of the ability to prepare a bibliography and notes, bearing in mind the golden rules of consistency and coherence, on which more can be found in subsections 3.4.7 and 3.4.8. If English is not your first language, be sure that you have someone to correct your text before you present it. In this way, you will be sure that you are really writing what you actually mean.

2.2 Essential components

The essential components of a seminar paper written on one author or upon a theme linking many authors are now given.

2.2.1

The frontispiece bears the title, the name of the student and the date and place. The title should be brief and pithy, in other words precise and crisp. Generally one is wise to leave devising the precise title until the work has been written.

Example A

PONTIFICAL INSTITUTE «REGINA MUNDI»

associated with the

PONTIFICAL GREGORIAN UNIVERSITY

TITLE

by

Name of Student

Year

Rome, Date

Title of course or seminar
Name of Professor

Example B

PONTIFICAL GREGORIAN UNIVERSITY

Faculty of Theology

TITLE OF ELABORATUM

Name of Professor
Name of course

Name of student
Matriculation number

Rome, Year

2.2.2

The table of abbreviations should be devised as in the example below. It should be noted that an abbreviation is italicized (or underlined) if it refers to a book title and not italicized if it refers to the authors.

ABBREVIATIONS

AAS = Acta Apostolicae Sedis. Commentarium officiale.
Rome: Vatican Polyglot Press, 1909–

CCC = *Catechism of the Catholic Church.*
Dublin: Veritas, 1994.

DP = *Discourses of the Popes from Pius XI to John Paul II to the Pontifical Academy of Sciences. 1936–1986.*
Vatican City: Pontifical Academy of Sciences, 1986.

DS = H. Denzinger and H. Schönmetzer. *Enchiridion Symbolorum, Definitionum et Declarationum de rebus fidei et morum.*
Barcelona/Freiburg im Breisgau/Rome: Herder, 1976.

IG = *Insegnamenti di Giovanni Paolo II.*
Vatican City: Vatican Polyglot Press, 1978– .

IP = *Insegnamenti di Paolo VI.* Vatican City: Vatican Polyglot Press, 1963–1978.

ND = J. Neuner and J. Dupuis, *The Christian Faith in the Doctrinal Documents of the Catholic Church.*
London: Collins, 1983.

OR = *L'Osservatore Romano*, daily Italian edition.

ORE = *L'Osservatore Romano*, weekly English edition.

PG = J. P. Migne. *Patrologiae cursus completus, series graeca.* 161 vols.
Paris: 1857–1866.

PL = J. P. Migne. *Patrologiae cursus completus, series latina.* 221 vols.
Paris: 1844–1864.

In the table of abbreviations, a statement of the following kind can be made:

The Scriptural quotations and abbreviations in this work are from the New Jerusalem Bible.

This statement implies that a consistent use is made of one version of the Bible throughout the work.

2.2.3
The table of contents which serves as a schematic summary of the work.

2.2.4
The introduction gives data about the author(s) studied along with a brief explanation of the background, as well as the limits and main sources used.

2.2.5
The central body of the text has headings which order the distribution of the material. The decimal method of division indicated below in chapter 3 (§3.3.3) for theses, is useful. Each heading should be short and to the point. Diagrams should be used in the text only if they serve a real purpose.

2.2.6
The conclusion sums up the main point of the work.

2.2.7
The essay should contain a number of quotes from the author(s) studied.

2.2.8
These quotations should be referenced with either footnotes or end notes, indicating sources or giving further information on the text. Chapter 4 should be consulted for information on how to make these.

2.2.9
An appendix may be employed if necessary.

2.2.10

The bibliography lists works consulted during research, divided according to primary and secondary sources. Chapter 5 should be consulted for information on how to do this.

Chapter 3

The Thesis

'True ease in writing comes from art, not chance,
As those move easiest who have learned to dance.'
Alexander Pope, *Essay on Criticism*

3.1 The choice of theme

3.1.1

The theme must lie within the general area of interest of the faculty in which the work is being carried out. If the faculty is Theology, then the topic should have a mainly theological slant. Similar considerations apply with Philosophy, Scripture, Canon Law, Ecclesiastical History, Spirituality, Patristics, Psychology, Social Sciences and so on. Interdisciplinary activity can be undertaken, but within well-defined parameters, otherwise the result is a vague piece of written work. In the search for a theme, one may begin from personal interest or from concrete and specific pastoral or missionary situations or else from scholarly discussions.

3.1.2

A thesis has a specific nature, which differs from that of a book, a lecture-course or a meditation. It is an exercise based on scientific research. Therefore, the theme should be restricted to a *limited* field which is precise in its scope. This must be borne in mind right from the start, so as to avoid the danger of not being able to explain the theme fully or else of falling into the trap of superficiality.

3.1.3

The thesis is based on scientific research, and it is not a meditation. Nevertheless, this does not exclude some degree of inspiration, reflection and personal interest. A thesis necessitates a good bibliography indicating sound sources and documents. However attractive a theme may be, it would be unwise to pursue it if there is insufficient material. Often personal interest in a theme must be balanced against the practicality of being able to carry it out. It is also necessary to weigh up whether there is sufficient material in the language in which the thesis will be written; otherwise, it will be necessary to translate large quantities of material, which is very time consuming.

3.1.4

The difference between a Master's thesis (or a Licence thesis) and a doctoral thesis should be borne in mind. Most universities stipulate a minimum and maximum length for a thesis. For a Master's or a Licence thesis the length is usually around 50–100 pages of double-spaced A4. For doctorates, at many universities the recommended length is often 200–300 pages of double-spaced A4. A careful check should be made to see whether the recommended length at the particular place of learning includes or excludes notes and bibliography. The purpose of a Master's (or a Licence) thesis is not the presentation of an original piece of work. Rather it is an exercise in the skills of research, in the use and organization of sources, and in the employment of a consistent form of methodology for citing sources and constructing a bibliography. In this sense, it is a preparation for a doctoral thesis. On the other hand, the doctoral dissertation involves in-depth investigation on one precise area, in such a way as to be a contribution to a greater understanding in that field. The originality may consist in the investigation of a new area, or a new look at an old question, or a panoramic view of a particular field taking a critical look at recent developments.

3.2 Starting research

3.2.1

At the beginning, it is advisable to have a provisional plan which serves to give direction to the research. This plan should have two characteristics:

a) It should be a simple guide and should combine intuitive and organizational aspects.
b) It is provisional, in that it will be progressively modified and deepened as the research proceeds. Thus it is almost always necessary to adapt the plan as the work proceeds.

3.2.2

It is important to know how to read the sources in order to seek and note the various possible relations of the text with the chosen theme. In this way the various facets of the theme are explored. The question which must be asked is: how does the text illustrate the particular chosen theme? At the same time, the thought of another author must not be forced so as to fit into the predetermined scheme of the thesis.

3.2.3

It is sometimes useful if one particular work (or series of works) lies at the heart of the inspiration of a thesis, but this kind of book is not always easy to find. In such a case, the student must scrupulously avoid merely copying the thought of the basic work. Rather, it is necessary to read the basic work many times so as to understand how some of its ideas may be woven into the thread of the thesis.

3.2.4

Of all the various stages in writing a thesis, namely collecting material, organizing the material, reflecting upon the material thus organized and collected, writing and re-writing, perhaps the most underestimated phase is that of *reflecting*. At this stage, nothing appears to be done, but like a seed buried deep in the earth, ideas are germinating. The work is like fine wine that is maturing. One friend even advised me to have a pen and paper ready at my bedside in case ideas occurred to me in the middle of the night!

3.2.5

During the reading process, it is important to have an effective way of taking notes. One way is the use of index-cards which was described in section 1.3.2. Here are some further hints on making notes using index cards:

a) The whole text should not be copied, but only those ideas or expressions which are particularly relevant to the theme. However, it is necessary to understand the thought of the author, and to summarize that thought.
b) Only one main idea should be put on each index card. An attempt should be made to cross reference ideas on the various index cards, so as to build up a relationship between them.
c) Complete bibliographical references should be taken for each text that is copied. This includes the surname and initial(s) of authors, full titles of books and articles, names and locations of publishing houses and full parameters of journals consulted. It is better to copy down too much concerning these parameters than too little. Often students and scholars have to return to sources at a later stage because of omissions earlier on; this is time-consuming as well as frustrating.

d) Personal reflections should be added on what is read, namely those reactions which the text inspires in the student. These ideas will often serve as a basis in the writing of the thesis.

3.3 A particular precise theme and a plan

3.3.1

There is a mutual relation between clarifying the theme and formulating the plan. Sometimes it is necessary to reformulate the theme to express the content more faithfully; however, it is also necessary to arrange the content so that it follows the theme. It should be borne in mind that, in many universities, there is provisional approval of a theme at the very start of research and then, a more definite approval once work has got under way and there is a solid chance of success. A theme which has been approved provisionally as an indication of a field of research can be reformulated or further specified according to the results of the research undertaken. The title of a thesis may even need slight modification as the research matures.

3.3.2 Characteristics of the plan:

Since the thesis must be a single unit, the plan must follow a dynamic and logical progression. Each chapter must be relevant to the overall theme, and each chapter must lead logically into the next one.

In order to develop the plan in this way, it is necessary to ask the questions: what do I intend to explain?; what is the basic thought or key idea that I wish to expose? The thesis must then be formed around this key idea.

A suitable division of chapters should be ensured. It should be kept in mind that in a Licence thesis of say 80 pages, 5 pages will go to the introduction and 5 to the conclusion. Then, a division could be made into three chapters of about 20 pages each or four chapters of about

15 pages. Each chapter of a thesis should contain *roughly* the same amount of material and thus each should be of similar length.

The plan, if efficiently made in the following way according to the order of the work, will then help greatly in dividing up the text.

3.3.3 The Order of the Work:

a) Frontispiece. Section §3.5 should be consulted for examples.
b) Table of Contents.
c) Preface: this is a personal approach to the thesis, and would include thanks and acknowledgements.
d) Table of Abbreviations: The principle is the same as the way it was done for seminar papers in chapter 2 (§2.2.2).
e) Introduction: this is the scientific beginning of the thesis.
f) The various chapters: each one should have a title which is short and encapsulates the content of the chapter in a pithy way.

The decimal division is a useful method and runs as follows:

Chapter 1
Section 1 is 1.1.
Subdivisions of this are 1.1.1, 1.1.2, 1.1.3 etc.
Section 2 is 1.2
Subdivisions of this are 1.2.1, 1.2.2, 1.2.3 etc.
Section 3 is 1.3
Subdivisions of this are 1.3.1, 1.3.2, 1.3.3 etc.
The same for other sections

Chapter 2
Section 1 is 2.1.
Subdivisions of this are 2.1.1, 2.1.2, 2.1.3 etc.
Section 2 is 2.2
Subdivisions of this are 2.2.1, 2.2.2, 2.2.3 etc.

Section 3 is 2.3
Subdivisions of this are 2.3.1, 2.3.2, 2.3.3 etc.
The same for other sections

Chapter 3
Section 1 is 3.1.
Subdivisions of this are 3.1.1, 3.1.2, 3.1.3 etc.
Section 2 is 3.2
Subdivisions of this are 3.2.1, 3.2.2, 3.2.3 etc.
Section 3 is 3.3
Subdivisions of this are 3.3.1, 3.3.2, 3.3.3 etc.
The same for other sections

The same principle is applied to each chapter; it is not necessary that each chapter have the same number of sections and sub-divisions.

g) References should be made according to the norms listed in chapter 4.
h) The Conclusion is the moment to draw together the main threads of the work and state what has been gained from doing it.
i) The Appendix, if it is necessary, is the part to include unpublished material (such as letters) for the reader's benefit. Of course, permission must be obtained from the owner of the material to do this.
j) A Glossary of terms may sometimes be useful, if these expressions have not been explained in the notes.
k) A Bibliography is constructed according to the rules given in chapter 5.
l) An Index can be made according to the directives given in §3.7.

3.4 Writing

This is the most creative phase of the work and depends on the personal contribution of each student. Some basic guidelines should be followed in the elaboration of the text.

3.4.1

It must not simply be a piece of patchwork, in which various interesting texts are sewn together with a bit of personal reflection. Rather, it should be a synthetic expression of personal thought. For this reason, care must be taken to avoid too many citations from authors. Quotations are meant to illustrate what you are saying, and should be like seasoning in food. Generally, quotations should not make up much more than 10% of the text. At some points in the text, more quotation may be necessary. At other points, like the introduction and conclusion, fewer citations will be needed.

3.4.2

The plan should be employed to ensure that one chapter flows logically into the next one so that the whole fits together in a coherent way. It is pertinent to remember what St. Thomas Aquinas said: 'Beauty includes three conditions, integrity or perfection; due proportion or harmony; and lastly, brightness, or clarity' (*Summa Theologiae* I, q.39, a.8). Thus, the thought should proceed logically and in an ordered fashion within each chapter. The discussion has to be unfolded with discipline. Unlike writing a book where there is more freedom, working on a thesis makes greater demands on formality. Sometimes it is necessary to move material from one chapter to another where it fits better. This process is rather like trying on clothes for size.

3.4.3

References with their footnotes or end notes are made according to the directives given below in chapter 4.

3.4.4

If English is not the first language of the writer of the thesis, the student should have someone whose first language is English to correct the text before it is finally presented. Lecturers or professors (even from other Universities) should not be asked to correct English in theses, because that is not their job, and also it introduces a possibility that they may help the candidate unduly in the formulation of the text. Rather the help should come from a friend or someone in the same religious community, or else a professional corrector.

3.4.5
Each paragraph should generally contain one main idea and should be neither too short nor too long. Each page should normally contain about two or three paragraphs. The main idea should be introduced at the beginning of the paragraph. Every new paragraph is indented about 5 spaces. The indentation should always be of the same length.

3.4.6
In the text or footnotes, a word or phrase should be *italicized* on computer programs which have this facility (or underlined on a typewriter):

(a) if it is foreign;
(b) if it is the title of a book, an official Church document, a journal or a film;
(c) if it is the proper name of a train, airplane or ship;
(d) if it needs emphasis.

Italics for emphasis should be used sparingly, otherwise the effect will be lost. Similarly, **bold print** for emphasis should also only used when really useful or necessary. Names of foreign organizations are written in Roman letters with initial capitals, like 'Pontificia Università Gregoriana'.

3.4.7
Consistency and coherence are very important in any piece of academic written work. An example lies in the

use of upper case and lower case. Either one or the other must be used consistently throughout the thesis. For example if 'Him' is used for God, then this must be done all the way through, with all other personal pronouns.

(a) Thus 'You' must be used for God instead of 'you'. Upper case must also be used for personal pronouns referring to Jesus Christ. It is incorrect and unacceptable to use upper case for personal pronouns referring to God and lower case for those referring to Jesus Christ. The choice of upper case also implies that, for example, Creation (the divine action), Incarnation, Resurrection, Ascension and Second Coming all commence with capital letters.
(b) Original sin need not be in upper case, however the Fall should be capitalized to indicate that it is not just any fall!
(c) Specific organizations and groups also take a capital letter, while general references do not. Thus, the East India Company, but a company.
(d) Geographical locations carry an initial capital when they are recognized regions. Thus, the Arun Valley, but the north-west.
(e) Historical periods of time are lower case if used in a general sense (e.g. medieval manuscripts) but upper case if they refer to a specific historical period (e.g. the High Middle Ages).
(f) Religious bodies carry an initial capital letter, where the reference is to an institution, for example Catholic, Catholicism, the Catholic Church.
(g) When ecclesiastical and noble titles are attached to the full title, they should always carry an initial capital letter. Thus, one should write Pope Urban VIII, the Queen of England, the Cardinal Archbishop of Westminster, the Duke of Kent. The same holds on other occasions when the titles are specific, such as the Pope, the Queen, the Cardinal, referring to a particular person. When the titles are general, they are in lower case, such as a queen, a cardinal, a

duke. However, some publishing houses would put a Pope in upper case even in general. A similar principle can be applied to councils. In general terms, an ecumenical council would be in lower case, but a specific case like the Second Vatican Council would be in upper case. Local councils follow the same principle, like the 11th Council of Toledo.

(h) The names of movements or styles usually take initial capitals when derived from proper nouns (such as Aristotelian, Thomistic, Romanesque) but otherwise begin in lower case (like baroque, imperialism, modernism).

3.4.8

Consistency should also be apparent in various other areas, which include the points in the following checklist:

(a) The method for making references (of which more will be said in chapter 4) and bibliographies (of which more in chapter 5), should be consistent.
(b) Verb endings should be checked for consistent use of '-ize' or '-ise'.
(c) A uniform choice for dates should be made between 15th September 1993 and September 15, 1993 or other methods.
(d) Numbers should generally be written in words below one hundred; above this the numerals should be written.
(e) Abbreviations should be made consistently with a table as in §2.2.2.
(f) Hyphenation and word-breaks should be made in a consistent way: most word-processing packages do this automatically.
(g) A decision should be made at the start of the work either for English or for American usage; this will govern spellings of words like 'colour' or 'color'.

3.4.9

While a great work of literature is rarely encountered in a thesis, certain *stylistic* hints should be borne in mind:

(a) Repetition of words or phrases should be avoided within a given paragraph. A thesaurus should be employed if necessary; many computer programs are equipped with one.
(b) Sentences should never begin with 'And', 'But' or with a numeral.
(c) The use of language should be optimized in order to convey the desired meaning in the minimum number of words.
(d) A check should be made to see if the expression is clear. It is wise to come back to the written work a couple of weeks after it has been written, in order to gain distance from it. Alternatively, the comments of a friend may be useful.
(e) Care should be taken to ensure that quotations really fit in with the flow of the text.
(f) The text should be even and consistent in its style; there should be no 'foreign bodies' of irrelevant material or embroidery in the writing. A thesis is not the same literary genre as a novel!

3.4.10

It is wise to write the first chapter, then hand it to the thesis director or moderator for comments. Then the same should be done with the second chapter and so on. The student should only return to the first chapter at the end, because then there will be an overview of the whole work, and one will see more clearly what changes are needed. The moderator may also suggest another approach. The adage that 'the art of writing is rewriting', should be borne in mind. Nevertheless, perfectionism should be avoided in a thesis which is an exercise, rather than a faultless finished product. An imperfect finished thesis is preferable to a hypothetically perfect work which is never completed.

3.5 Frontispieces

The frontispiece should contain the following information:

(a) the name of the university and the faculty;
(b) the title of the thesis;
(c) the name of the author;
(d) the name of the moderator or director of the thesis and sometimes the second readers according to the norms of the particular university;
(e) the city and year of publication.

Here are some examples of frontispieces:

3.5.1 Master of Arts in Religious Sciences at the Pontifical Institute «Regina Mundi»:

PONTIFICAL INSTITUTE «REGINA MUNDI»

ASSOCIATED WITH THE

PONTIFICAL GREGORIAN UNIVERSITY

THESIS FOR THE

MASTER OF ARTS IN RELIGIOUS SCIENCES

DIALOGUE BETWEEN CHRISTIAN FAITH AND NATURAL SCIENCE

IN THE WORKS OF

RECENT WRITERS

by

Sr. Joan Smith

Director: Fr. John Brown

Rome, May 1996

3.5.2 Licence thesis at the Pontifical Gregorian University:

PONTIFICAL GREGORIAN UNIVERSITY

Faculty of Theology

FAITH AND SCIENCE

SINCE

GAUDIUM ET SPES

Tesina for the Licentiate

in Fundamental theology

presented to

Fr. Gerald O'Collins S.J.

by

Fr. Paul Haffner

(Venerable English College)

Rome, 22 February 1982

3.5.3 Doctoral thesis in theology at the Pontifical Gregorian University:

PONTIFICIA UNIVERSITA GREGORIANA

Facultas Theologiae

Paul Haffner

CHRISTIAN FAITH IN GOD THE CREATOR

IN RELATION TO MODERN SCIENCE

ACCORDING TO THE WORKS OF

STANLEY L. JAKI

Dissertatio ad Doctoratum

Moderator: R.P. Willibrord Welten, S.I.

Roma 1987

3.5.4 Doctoral thesis in philosophy at the Pontifical Urban University:

PONTIFICIA UNIVERSITAS URBANIANA

Facoltà di Filosofia

Title of thesis

Name of student

Tesi di Laurea in Filosofia

Moderatore: Professor.................................

Correlatori: 1. Professor...............................

2. Professor...............................

City

Year

3.5.5 Doctoral thesis in Canon Law at the Angelicum University:

PONTIFICIA STUDIORUM UNIVERSITATIS
S.THOMAE IN URBE

Facultas Iuris Canonici

Fred A. Jones

A NEW STUDY

CONCERNING FEAST DAYS

ACCORDING TO CANON 1246 §1

Historico-theological and canonical aspects

(Dissertatio ad Doctoratum)

Moderator: John G. Smith, O.P.

Roma 1991

3.6 Numbering the pages

It is important to ensure consistency in the process of numbering the pages of the thesis. The first two pages which are blank are counted for the purposes of page numbering, even though no number actually appears on them. The frontispiece also counts as two page numbers, even though no number actually appears on it. The table of contents which then follows is numbered as either -5- or preferably -v-. Generally it is better to use Roman numerals for the part of the thesis lying before the text itself. Thus the Preface, Forward and Abbreviations pages are numbered in Roman numerals. The text itself then begins in Arabic numerals at -1-. Each new chapter (and the Bibliography, Appendix and Index) begins on a new odd-numbered page.

3.7 Making an Index

3.7.1

This is a useful optional extra for a doctorate thesis. Only the text proper with its references is indexed. Forewords, Prefaces, and Bibliographies are not indexed. It is possible to make an index of names and a separate index of subjects, or else a combined index. Consistency should be ensured in the use of alphabetical order as regards peoples' names; more on this can be seen in section 5.1.

3.7.2

In constructing the index, either a computer program should be used or the following method, with a *copy* of the typescript.

(a) On the duplicate manuscript are highlighted (e.g. by coloured underlinings), right from the moment of writing the first chapter, the names or key words or phrases that are chosen for the index entries.

(b) The entries are written on filing cards or uniform slips of paper, one card or slip per entry, noting the typescript page number on each entry in pencil.
(c) The cards or slips are kept in the order in which the entries appear in the typescript (and are numbered consecutively, in case they are accidentally disordered) until the final version of the thesis is ready.
(d) The cards or slips are processed with the final version of the thesis, and the final page references are inserted in pen on the cards or slips in place of the pencilled ones.
(e) Only after the page-numbers of the final typescript have been inserted are the slips put in alphabetical order, any duplicates removed and entries combined where necessary.
(f) Finally, the index is typed out in single columns, double-spaced, on one side only of each sheet.

3.8 Handing in the finished product

3.8.1

The thesis should be handed in to the appropriate body in the university (often the Secretariat) within the deadline which is normally allowed. The deadline is often designed to give the examiners a chance to read and evaluate the work before the defence.

3.8.2

It should be ensured that the thesis has the correct size and the correct binding for the norms of the particular university. The binding must often be of a specific colour. The stipulated number of typewritten and bound copies must be handed in, and, of course, the candidate should keep a copy. The personal copy will help in the formulation of the presentation for the defence.

3.9 The defence

Normally, a public defence lasts just over one hour. The candidate should bear in mind that he or she has all but obtained the academic title by this stage, so that this session should be viewed more as an opportunity to present the results to the public, often including family and friends, rather than as a gruelling examination. In the first 20 minutes or so, the candidate usually offers a synthesis of his or her dissertation and briefly presents the reasons for the choice of the theme, the particular difficulties encountered, and the originality and importance of the work. Finally the conclusions are presented. In the remaining period, the examiners question the candidate in turn, in such a way as to highlight important aspects of the work, to shed light on obscure details or to seek clarification of certain points.

3.10 Publication

Publication of the whole or a part of the thesis after the defence constitutes the final exercise required for obtaining the title of Doctor in a particular discipline. After the defence, the examiners usually furnish a series of directives as to what further work (if any) needs to be done before the whole thesis or a suitable extract can be published. Having followed their suggestions, the candidate then prepares the text for publication, which usually involves a private printing operation by offset or publication of an excerpt in a learned journal. If the candidate prints the thesis privately in whole or part, he or she should adhere carefully to the norms of the university regarding the format, the frontispiece and the number of copies which must be handed in to the relevant authorities. In an ecclesiastical faculty, the *Imprimatur* and *Nihil obstat*, as an expression that the work is free from doctrinal or moral error, usually need to be obtained from the relevant authority prior to publication. Furthermore, it is wise to publish the thesis as soon as possible after the defence, while it is still fresh in the mind. Also, some universities require that, once a certain period of time has elapsed after the defence, a thesis must be re-submitted to its board of censors for a new approval before publication.

Chapter 4

References

'Notes are often necessary, but they are necessary evils.'

Samuel Johnson, *Shakespeare*

The present chapter deals with the mechanics of making notes for both seminar and scientific papers and for theses. This method can also be used when writing a book in some academic field.

4.1 Making quotations

4.1.1 Direct quotation

With a direct quotation it is necessary to copy what an author has said 'word for word'. A long direct quotation has to placed on its own, otherwise it would be lost in the text. Thus, if the quotation is 5 lines or less in length, it is put in inverted commas in the text: if longer than 5 lines, it is put in an indented single-spaced section on its own. With a direct quotation, it is necessary to copy *exactly* what the author has said, even if there is a mistake in spelling or syntax. Any mistake in a quoted text should be indicated with the expression (*sic*). This protects the writer of a thesis from critics who may otherwise think that the error was made in copying the passage.

Examples of direct quotations:

(a) *5 lines or shorter*:

Particularly over the past thirty years, the mass media have been featuring almost daily the various warning signs in the current environmental crisis. Among these are the problem of deforestation and the disappearance of various animal species. There is air pollution (for example from car-exhausts), sea pollution (from petrol discharged accidentally by ships) and ground pollution (from chemical wastes, for instance). Big cities are inundated with refuse, while special difficulties are encountered in the disposal of nuclear waste. There is the whole question of the destruction of the ozone layer by fluorocarbons. These and other problems are the result of the intervention of man in the macro-environment of nature. However, man also interferes in the genetic micro-environment of cells of living organisms so provoking various undesirable effects. Our Holy Father, Pope John Paul II in his message for peace of 1 January 1990 declared that 'we are not yet in a position to assess the biological disturbance that could result from the unscrupulous development of new forms of plant and animal life, to say nothing of unacceptable experimentation regarding the origins of human life itself.'[2]

---

2. Pope John Paul II, *Peace with God the Creator, Peace with All of Creation*, Message for World Day of Peace 1990, §7.3.

(b) *longer than five lines*:

The healing-process of the entire cosmos is one which takes place slowly and silently. It finds its origin in Christ's redemptive act and began on the morning of Easter Sunday, as G. K. Chesterton powerfully illustrated:

On the third day the friends of Christ coming at daybreak to the place found the grave empty and the stone rolled away. In varying ways they realised the new wonder; but even they hardly realised that the world had died in the night. What they were looking at was the first day of a new creation, with a new heaven and a new earth; and in a semblance of the gardener God walked again in a garden, in the cool not of the evening but the dawn.[2]

2. G. K. Chesterton, *The Everlasting Man* (Garden City, New York: Image Books, 1955), pp.216-217.

4.1.2 Indirect quotation

With an indirect quotation, the citation quoted in the main body of the text is not direct, and is therefore not put in quotation marks and thus, in the note, indirectness of the quote is indicated by using Cf. (=confer). Cf. is used whenever it is desired to acknowledge a debt to someone else's thought, however remotely. Instead of Cf. it is also possible to use 'See'. Cf. is used when making a paraphrase of an author's thought or expressing a debt for a single idea or multiple ideas. Cf. or 'See' may be used to refer to points made earlier or later in the thesis. 'Cf.p.15 above' refers to an earlier point and 'Cf.p. 267 below' refers to a later point.

Example of indirect quotation:

Particularly over the past thirty years, the mass media have been featuring almost daily the various warning signs in the current environmental crisis. Among these are the problem of deforestation and the disappearance of various animal species. There is air pollution (for example from car-exhausts), sea pollution (from petrol discharged accidentally by ships) and ground pollution (from chemical wastes, for instance). Big cities are inundated with refuse, while special difficulties are encountered in the disposal of nuclear waste. There is the whole question of the destruction of the ozone layer by fluorocarbons. These and other problems are the result of the intervention of man in the macro-environment of nature. However, man also interferes in the genetic micro-environment of cells of living organisms so provoking various undesirable effects. Our Holy Father, Pope John Paul II in his message for peace of 1 January 1990 pointed out the dangers involved in a manipulation of the origins of human life.[2]

---

2. Cf. Pope John Paul II, *Peace with God the Creator, Peace with all of Creation,* Message for World Day of Peace 1990, §7.3.

4.1.3

References are also used to give further, more detailed information illustrating points made in the text. This information would interrupt the flow if placed in the main body of the thesis, but in a note the reader can refer to it when he or she wants.

4.1.4

If the translation of some author is quoted in the thesis, the text in its original language can be furnished in the note, if it sheds some particular light on the discussion. In this way, the thesis should be written exclusively in one language for tidiness, and any original foreign words are then put in the notes. It is necessary to state who is responsible for the translation. If the writer of the thesis is responsible, then in a note the expression "translation mine" should be used. If just a single foreign word appears in the text, it is sufficient to put the translation alongside it in brackets.

4.1.5

In the case of a quotation within a quotation, the 'inner' citation must be distinguished from the outer one by means of either (a) a different type of quotation marks, for example, '' as opposed to " " or else (b) by triangular brackets, like this « ».

Example:

P. Haffner states that 'one such cosmologist is S. Weinberg who wrote: «I cannot deny a feeling of unreality in writing about the first three minutes as if we really know what we are talking about.»'[2]

---

2. P. Haffner, *Creation and Scientific Creativity* (Front Royal: Christendom Press, 1991), p.93. Cf. S. Weinberg, *The First Three Minutes: A Modern View of the Universe* (London: André Deutsch, 1970), p.7

4.1.6

Concerning quotations and punctuation, care should be exercised to be correct and consistent. A *comma* within a quoted text generally falls inside the quotation marks because it is part of the text, thus:

> 'The ultimate synthesis,' Jaki notes, 'the rock-bottom layer of the material world, is today as far away as it has ever been.'

The *full-stop* should also generally be put within the quotation marks as in the example above. However, many publications use a more refined approach, based on the so-called Hart's Rules. These rules regulate that punctuation which *actually belongs to the cited text* falls inside the quotation marks, while the other punctuation should remain outside. These rules indicate that where a full sentence, with an initial capital letter, is quoted at the end of the sentence, the full stop precedes the inverted commas. In all other instances, when only a phrase is quoted, the full-stop should follow the inverted commas. Other punctuation marks are placed in relation to quotation marks according to sense.

Examples:

1) He said: 'It is an excellent idea.'
2) He said it was 'an excellent idea'.
3) 'It is', he said, 'an excellent idea.'
4) 'It is,' he said, 'for the most part, an excellent idea.'

Where words are omitted from a cited passage, three spaced dots are used to indicate this fact. A full stop should be added after a completed sentence.

Examples:

1) 'Christ ... fulfils this prophetic office, not only by the hierarchy ... but also by the laity.'
2) 'The most important member is Christ, since He is the Head .... Therefore the riches of Christ are communicated to all the members.'

4.1.7

If, in a quotation, a word or phrase is italicized which the author did not so emphasize, this fact should be indicated with the expression [italics mine] in the note corresponding to the quotation.

4.2 References with examples

4.2.1

Scripture quotations can generally be left in the text in brackets, using the standard abbreviations for the books of the Bible. The method recommended is to give the book of the Bible, followed by the chapter, then a colon and then the verse. Various quotations from the same book and chapter are separated by a comma and citations from different chapters or books are separated by a semicolon. Hence the reference (Rev 21:1, 5–6) means the book of Revelation chapter 21 verses 1 and 5 to 6. The indication (Pr 9:1; Ws 7:27) invites the reader to consult the book of Proverbs chapter 9 verse 1 and the book of Wisdom chapter 7 verse 27. It should be ensured that in any one given piece of written work one consistent system of Scriptural abbreviations be followed. All other quotations should be generally be referenced. In the case of a Scripture reference, a particular application is made of rule 4.1.6, and the full stop is put beyond the bracketed reference.

Example:

'The spirit of the Lord, indeed fills the whole world, and that which holds all things together knows every word that is said' (Ws 1:7).

If there is a question mark or an exclamation mark at the end of the Scriptural passage, a full stop can be added after the bracketed reference so as not to leave it 'hanging in the air' between two sentences.

Example:

'When I gave the earth shape, did anyone help me?' (Is 44:24).

4.2.2

Within the body of the text, references are numbered in sequence. A sequential numbering distinguishes the present method from that used in the natural sciences, where the numbers in the text are not in numerical order as they refer variously to the bibliography which is in numerical order. At least from an aesthetic point of view the present author feels that a sequential numbering in the text is preferable. The reference is indicated by a printed number at the end of the passage to which it refers. This number always comes *after* any punctuation. For an article, essay or term paper, the numbering continues from beginning to end. In a thesis or a book, numbering of references should begin again with each chapter. References are then indicated either with *footnotes* or with *end notes*.

(a) Footnotes should be at the bottom of the text and they should follow each other sequentially in numerical order on the page. Each reference number always corresponds to a footnote with the same number at the bottom of the page. Care should be taken that the footnote appears on the same page as the reference to which it is attached. A fundamental principle of scholarly work is that each page should be complete in itself. Some computer programs may have difficulty in achieving this, but at least it should be ensured that even a long footnote begins on the page to which it refers. The beginning of the footnotes should be separated from the text by typing an unbroken line of length about twenty spaces, and then after a space, the footnotes begin. Many word-processing computer programs make footnotes automatically.

(b) An end note is placed at the end of a document. In a paper, this means at the end of the paper. With a thesis, many universities only allow end notes if these are bound in a separate volume. It is wise to check the particular regulations of the relevant university before embarking on a choice between footnotes and end notes.

4.2.3

The actual text of footnotes and end notes should be single-spaced, but there should be double spacing between notes.

4.2.4

Where two or more quotations in succession are from the same source and the same page, it is advisable to cover them all under a single reference. It is also *possible* to do this if the quotations are taken from different pages, but, in this case it is not always clear to the reader exactly what comes from where. Thus, in this latter situation, the pages must be cited in order of appearance.

Example:

'The ultimate synthesis,' Jaki notes, 'the rock-bottom layer of the material world, is today as far away as it has ever been.' However he qualifies this, lest he appear to support a sort of agnostic scepticism, by adding that 'the kernel of scientific truth will become better defined as time goes on.'[2]

---

2. S. L. Jaki, *The Relevance of Physics* (Edinburgh: Scottish Academic Press, ^{2}1992) pp.187, 137.

Note that the superscript '2' before the date of publication indicates the 2nd edition of the book.

4.2.5 Footnote or End note forms:

The principle in each case is to specify the document in such a way that it cannot in any fashion be confused with any other similar document. The idea here is that the writer of a thesis is making his or her own life a little more difficult in order to make it easier for the reader! It is preferable to avoid the use of expressions involving f. and ff. like p.5f. (meaning page 5 and the page following) and p.5ff. (meaning page 5 and the pages following). The pages should be cited specifically.

A) Document of the Magisterium

The name of the Pope, Vatican department, Council or bishop should be given and then the type and name of the document, followed by the section number. Usually, section numbers are given in Vatican documents. This is much more useful than page numbers as these latter differ according to the language edition and according to the translation.

Examples:

---

1. Second Vatican Council, Dogmatic Constitution on the Church *Lumen Gentium,* §10.

If this document were cited many times, it could be suitably abbreviated (and then it must appear in the table of abbreviations as in §2.2.2) so that the note would simply read:

---

1. LG 10.

---

2. Pope John Paul II, Apostolic Letter *Mulieris Dignitatem* §7.3.

The subdivision 7.3 is useful. It means the third paragraph in the section officially numbered 7.

Remember that, when making a citation from an ecclesiastical document, it is insufficient to put simply a reference to a collection thus, DS 1638. The source must be stated, thus: Council of Trent, Session XIII, *Decree on the Most Holy Eucharist*, Chapter II as found in DS 1638.

****

B) Book with one author:

The initial(s) and surname of the author must be given. It is preferable just to cite the initials rather than the full Christian name as the latter may not always be easy to find. In any case, consistency would not allow the use sometimes of full Christian names and sometimes of initials. Then the title and sub-title of the book duly italicized, the place of publication (city and publishing house) and the date of publication should be given. The page number(s) are then listed.

Example:

---

1. P. Haffner, *Creation and Scientific Creativity: A Study in the Thought of S. L. Jaki* (Front Royal: Christendom Press, 1991), p.70.

****

C) Book with two authors:

The initials and names of the authors must be given, the title of the book, the place of publication (city and publishing house) and the date of publication. The page number(s) are then listed. The order of authors' names must be given exactly as printed in the title page of the book.

Example:

---

1. J. D. Barrow and F. J. Tipler, *The Anthropic Cosmological Principle* (Oxford: Clarendon Press, 1986), pp.79–80.

****

D) Book with many authors:

When dealing with a book with more than three authors, instead of the names of the authors, AA.VV. (which means various authors), should be written. Then, the title of the book, the place of publication (city and publishing house) and the date of publication are given. The page number(s) are then cited as usual. In the case where a particular editor is responsible for this kind of volume, his or her name should be cited. Remember that if a passage from an article by one author within a collection is cited, this author should be named first in the note. Thus, a clear distinction is made between a collection of essays in which each author is responsible for one part and a volume in which all the authors have written the whole.

Examples:

---

1. Pope John XXIII, *Discourse to the Pontifical Academy of Sciences,* 30th October 1961 in AA.VV. *Discourses of the Popes from Pius XI to John Paul II to the Pontifical Academy of Sciences. 1936–1986* (Vatican City: Pontifical Academy of Sciences, 1986), p.103.

---

2. P. Poupard(ed.). *Science et Foi* (Tournai: Desclée, 1982), p.78.

---

3. O. Pedersen, 'Christian Belief and the Fascination of Science' in R. J. Russell, W. R. Stoeger, and G. V. Coyne (eds.) *Physics, Philosophy, and Theology: A Common Quest for Understanding* (Vatican City State: Vatican Observatory, 1988), p.126.

****

E) Article in a periodical:

The initial(s) and name of the author must be given, the title of the article in inverted commas, the title of the periodical duly italicized, specifying also the volume number and year of the periodical. Sometimes, if the journal has pages which begin again for every month or every issue of a given year, it is also necessary to give the number which specifies the particular issue within a given year: e.g. 17/1, where '17' is the volume number and '1' is the issue number. If the periodical is published in more than one language edition or has a name that could be confused with another journal, the place of publication should be indicated in brackets after the name of the periodical. The page number(s) are then listed.

Example:

---

1. J. Cardinal Ratzinger, 'Jesus Christ today' in *Communio* (Notre Dame) 17/1 (1990), pp.68–69.

****

F) Article in a newspaper:

The initial(s) and name of the author must be given, the title of the article in inverted commas, the title of the newspaper duly italicized, specifying also the precise date on which it appeared (day/month/year). The page number(s) are then specified.

Example:

---

1. P. E. Hodgson, 'A Duty to Share Knowledge' in *The Times* (27 April 1985), p.10.

****

G) Article in an encyclopaedia/biblical commentary/ dictionary:

The initial(s) and name of the author must be given, the title of the article in inverted commas, the title of the encyclopaedia duly italicized, specifying also the volume number and place and year of publication. The page(s) are then listed.

Example:

---

1. F. D. Wilhelmsen, 'Realism' in *New Catholic Encyclopaedia* (New York: McGraw Hill, 1967) Volume 12, pp.110–111.

****

H) A book review:

The writer of the book review must be specified, the title of the review (if applicable), and then the name of the author of the book reviewed, the title and details of the book and also where the review was published.

Example:

---

1. P. M. Haffner, review of S. L. Jaki, *Chance or Reality and Other Essays* (Lanham: University Press of America, 1986) in *Gregorianum* 89(1988), p.598.

****

I) A Poem:

The initial(s) and name of the author must be given, the title of the poem in inverted commas, the title of the collection (duly italicized) in which it was found with the name of the editor, and the place and year of publication. The page number(s) are then listed. In addition, a line number (abbreviated by l.) can be given for a poem.

Example:

---

1. G. M. Hopkins, 'The furl of fresh-leaved dogrose' l.4, in *Poems by Gerard Manley Hopkins*, (ed. N. H. Mackenzie) (London: The Folio Society, 1974), p.79.

****

J) A Song:

The initial (s) and name of the author must be given, the title of the song in inverted commas, the title of the collection or album in which it was found with the name of the publisher, and the place and year of publication. The songwriter is sometimes not the same person as the singer. It should be stated if the author is anonymous.

Example:

---

1. C. de Burgh, 'The Spirit of Man' in *Into the Light* (London: A & M Records, 1986).

****

K) A Film:

If a film is mentioned in the notes, it should be specified by the title (italicized), the main country of production, the company which made it and the year.

Example:

---

1. *Angels* (USA: Walt Disney, 1994).

****

L) Archive Material:

Here, the nature of the document must be indicated and the relevant date. The archives of the pertinent institution should then be specified and finally the parameters which locate it in that particular archive as was seen in §1.1.2.

Examples:

---

1. Letter of Cardinal John Smith to Bishop Fred Jones, 28 September 1979. Archives of the Pontifical Council for General Welfare Protocol N° 679/79; Position 401.

---

2. British Library, Additional MSS 410, ff. 7–9; 912, f. 10.

****

M) Unpublished material:

The author of the material should be mentioned, the place where and the date when it was written (so that it can be located, for example in a university library) as well as the fact that it is unpublished.

Example:

---

1. V. Hartley von Knieriem, unpublished thesis *Towards a Theology of Woman according to Paul Evdokimov* (Rome: Pontifical Institute Regina Mundi, 1995), p.45.

N) An Interview:

The name of the person interviewed should be mentioned, the date on which the interview took place, and also the medium on which it was recorded.

Example:

---

1. Interview with Rt. Rev. John Smith, Bishop of Appleford, 25th May 1989. Transcribed from audio-tape.

****

Further applications to other cases can be made using a development of the method used in the above examples.

4.3 Repeating quotes

4.3.1 When to use *ibid*:

a *Ibid.* is an abbreviation for *ibidem* which means 'in the same place.' It is used when references to the same work follow one another without any intervening reference.

b) *Ibid.* is used without any page number when the reference is found on the same page as the page reference immediately previous. A simple use is made of *ibid.* plus the page number if the page number is different from the previous reference.

Example:

---

1. E. L. Mascall, *Christian Theology and Natural Science* (London: Longmans Green and Co, 1957), p.41.
2. *Ibid.*, p.45.
3. *Ibid.*

4.3.2 When not to use *ibid*:

a) Never use *ibid* when referring to another work by the same author. In this case Idem (meaning 'the same') must be employed, followed by the name of the work. For more than one author Iidem is used and for an authoress, Eadem. Although Idem is a Latin word, it is not italicized so as to distinguish it from *ibid.*, which refers to a work.

Example:

---

1. S. L. Jaki, *Cosmos and Creator* (Edinburgh: Scottish Academic Press, 1980), p.65.

2. Idem, *Is There a Universe?* (Liverpool: University Press, 1993), p.70.

****

b) Never use *ibid.* when there is an intervening reference between notes even though the reference has already been cited in full previously. In this case, the surname of the author may be used (omitting his/her initials unless another author in the thesis has the same surname), with a shortened form of the work and the page number.

Example:

---

1. P. Haffner, *Creation and Scientific Creativity: A Study in the Thought of S. L. Jaki* (Front Royal: Christendom Press, 1991), p.70.

2. S. L. Jaki, *Cosmos and Creator* (Edinburgh: Scottish Academic Press, 1980), p.65.

3. Idem, *Is There a Universe?* (Liverpool: University Press, 1993), p.70.

4. Haffner, *Creation and Scientific Creativity*, p.70.

c) Never use *ibid.* when there are two references in the preceding note, as it will not be clear which one is being referred to. In this case, the successive reference must be written in full or in abbreviated form, thus:

---

1. S. L. Jaki, *The Savior of Science* (Washington, D.C.: Regnery Gateway, 1988), p.199 and idem, *The Purpose of It All* (Edinburgh: Scottish Academic Press, 1990), p.144.

2. Jaki, *The Purpose of It All*, pp. 141–144.

4.3.3 When to use *op. cit.*:

The expression *op. cit.* stands for *opus citatum*, meaning 'the work quoted.' This may be used in the case of an author of whom only one work is being considered in the entire thesis. Then the work may be quoted in full the first time it is mentioned and thereafter *op. cit.* may be used. Some scholars also use the expression to stand for a title of a book which has been mentioned in the immediately preceding reference. If an author with several works is mentioned in the thesis, the first time an author is mentioned, each work should be cited in full. On subsequent occasions, only the surname of the author and an abbreviated version of his or her work are given as described in §4.3.2, thus avoiding the use of *op. cit.*

4.3.4 When to use *loc. cit.*:

The expression *loc. cit.* stands for *locus citatus*, meaning 'the place quoted.' The expression should only be used to replace quoting in full or abbreviated form the place where a quotation has been found, if there is no danger of confusion. Some scholars use it to stand for a title of an encyclopaedia or large reference work, or a page number which has been mentioned in the immediately preceding reference. This may not always be completely clear. It is, of course, possible to make references without the use of *op. cit.* and *loc. cit.* and many scholars prefer to avoid these expressions. If the method of abbreviating works laid out in §4.3.2 is employed, that system should not be mixed with a use of *op. cit.* and *loc. cit.*, because this shows a lack of economy. It is better to avoid superfluous expressions as far as possible.

4.4 Frequent mistakes

4.4.1 Failure to distinguish between primary and secondary sources:

Quoting St. Augustine, Pope John Paul II states that the Eucharist in the Church is 'the Sacrament of piety, the Sign of unity and the Bond of charity.'[2]

---

2. Pope John Paul II, *Dominicae Coenae* § 13.5

The mistake is that St. Augustine should also have been mentioned in the note. So the correct way to make the note would have been:

---

2. Pope John Paul II, *Dominicae Coenae* § 13.5. See St. Augustine, *In Evangelium Ioannis tractatus* 26, 13. *PL* 35, 1613.

4.4.2 Failure to cite primary source:

As Jaki states: 'Without Creation, and a Creation by God who is Father, there is no possibility of a discourse about Incarnation, Redemption, and final Consummation in a New Heaven and earth, the great prophecy of the Creed.'[2]

---

2. P. Haffner, *Creation and Scientific Creativity: A Study in the Thought of S. L. Jaki* (Front Royal, Va.: Christendom Press, 1991), p.61.

The *primary source* should have been put in the note and *not* the secondary source.

The note should have read:

---

2. S. L. Jaki, *Cosmos and Creator* (Edinburgh: Scottish Academic Press, 1980), p.56.

Chapter 5

Bibliography

'Thousands kiss the book's outside who ne'er look within.'

William Cowper, *Expostulation*

5.1 Rules for alphabetical order

Making a bibliography is based upon arranging titles in alphabetical or chronological order. Here are some fundamental rules about arranging names in alphabetical order:

5.1.1

In the case of two authors having the same surname with the same initial, for example, John SMITH and Jean SMITH, the Christian names must be cited in full as these are used as a criterion to give precedence to Jean Smith.
SMITH, Jean
SMITH, John

If the initials are not the same, it should be clear that C. Smith has alphabetic precedence over C. A. Smith, and that C. A. Smith has alphabetic precedence over C. B. Smith.

5.1.2
It is important to know how to treat the case of letters which have signs connected with them such as:

é, è, ù, ç, ü, ö, ä, â, ê, ô, å, ñ.

These letters are considered for classification as if they did not have any sign. Thus Döllinger is placed after Dolcetto.

5.1.3
In the case of names with a particle indicating the name of the father or the clan, apostrophes are disregarded in placing the allocation of alphabetical order.

John McDermott goes under **M**, but is placed after Philip MacLean.

Daniel O'Grady goes under **O**.

Michael ApRoberts goes under **A**.

Angela FitzHerbert goes under **F**.

5.1.4 Titles
Titles of sanctity or of ecclesiastical or civil rank do not affect alphabetical order.
Thus: Pope Saint Gregory the Great goes under **G**
Blessed Bishop Niels Stensen goes under **S**.
Sir Isaac Newton goes under **N**.

5.1.5 Noble names and others formed by articles and prepositions:
The rule is that such articles and prepositions do not determine alphabetical order.
Thus:
Hans Urs von Balthasar goes under **B**.
Ignace de la Potterie goes under **P**.

However, Richard Van Dyck goes under **V** because the word 'Van' begins with a capital letter, is not a preposition, and is thus considered part of the surname.

A further exception is that in Italy, articles and prepositions do determine alphabetical order. Hence F. de Santis precedes G. de Santo, but both are listed under the letter **D**.

5.1.5 For double-barrelled names:
There is an international rule which stipulates that generally the first significant surname governs alphabetical order, whether there is hyphenation or not. Care should be taken however, since while in Spain the first surname is important for alphabetical order, in Portugal the last surname name gives the order.
Thus:
H. Hamilton-Dalrymple goes under **H**.
C. Maxwell Stewart goes under **M**.
(It should be clear that J. Maxwell has alphabetic precedence over C. Maxwell Stewart.)

M. Schmidt von Braun goes under **S**.

However, D. N. Queiroz de Barros da Cunha, a Portuguese name, goes under **C**, because in Portugal the last surname is determinant of alphabetical order.

5.2 Examples

Titles of books must be put exactly as they are to be found in the original frontispiece. A distinction should be made between primary sources, which constitute the work of a particular author, and secondary sources which consist of what someone else has written about this author. Thus, within the following headings the bibliography can be further divided according to the criteria of primary and secondary sources.

A. Sacred Scripture:
It is neither necessary nor sufficient to simply write the Bible under this heading, because it is clear that in any

theological work, the Bible will play some part! In fact, in a thesis which is not specifically specialized in Scripture, the particular version of the Bible which has been used should have already been mentioned in the Table of Abbreviations (see §2.2.2). The Scriptural bibliography as such should be subdivided according to critical editions, synopses, dictionaries, concordances and translations of Scripture. The author(s), the titles (duly italicized) the place(s) and date of publication should be indicated. Next to the publication date, a superscript number indicates the edition. Under each subheading, the titles should be arranged alphabetically according to the surname of the principal author. For several works by the same author, the arrangement is chronological, with the oldest listed first. An often repeated source can simply be put in the Table of Abbreviations. For further ideas on how to organize a Scriptural bibliography for a thesis in a biblical specialization, the student should consult:

Elenchus Bibliographicus Biblicus of Biblica. Rome: Biblical Institute Press. 65 volumes up to 1984.

Elenchus of Biblica. Roma: Editrice Pontificio Istituto Biblico. 8 volumes up to 1995.

Examples:

Critical Editions:

Aland, K., Black, M., Martini, C. M., Metzger, B. M., Wikgren, A. *The Greek New Testament*. New York/London/Edinburgh/Amsterdam/Stuttgart: 1975^{3}.

Nestle, E. and Aland, K. *Novum Testamentum graece et latine*. Stuttgart: 1963^{25}.

Biblical dictionaries:

Douglas, J. D., and Tanney Merrill, C. *The NIV compact dictionary of the Bible*. Grand Rapids: Zondervan, 1989.

Green, J. B., McKnight, S., Marshall, I. H. *Dictionary of Jesus and the Gospels*. Leicester: Intervarsity Press, 1992.

Hennig, K. *Jerusalemer Bibel-Lexikon*. Stu-Neuhausen: Hänssler, 1989.

B. The Magisterium:

Documents of the Magisterium are arranged in the following order:

First any collections of documents. Well-known and often-used collections of Papal documents like those arranged by Neuner and Dupuis or Denzinger and Schönmetzer should not be placed here, but rather should go in the table of abbreviations.

Then, Papal documents in are placed in chronological order, oldest first, so that the bibliography follows an historical order. For each Pope, the documents in are arranged in chronological order, oldest first.

Example:

AA.VV.	*Discourses of the Popes from Pius XI to John Paul II to the Pontifical Academy of Sciences. 1936–1986.* English edition edited by Fr. Paul Haffner. Pontificiae Academiae Scientiarum Scripta Varia 66. Vatican City: Pontificia Academia Scientiarum, 1986.
Pope Pius XI.	Motu Proprio *In multis solaciis. AAS* 28 (1936) pp.421–424.
Pope Pius XII.	*Allocutio — iis qui interfuerunt Conventui universali de Astronomia, Romae habito. AAS* 44 (1952) pp.732–739.
Pope Paul VI.	*Credo of the People of God.* 30 June 1986. Introduction, para 5. *AAS* 60 (1968) p.435.

————	*Allocution on the Apollo 10 Mission.* 21 May 1969. *IP* 7 (1969) pp.489–492.
————	*Allocution at General Audience.* 9 February 1977. *IP* 15 (1977) pp.141–143.
Pope John Paul II.	Encyclical Letter *Redemptor Hominis.* 4 March 1979. *IG* 2/1 (1979) pp.550–609.

****

C. Encyclopaedias and Dictionaries:
If the works are specifically Scriptural or relate to the Magisterium, they should be gathered, in alphabetical order, under headings A or B above respectively, under an appropriate sub-heading of encyclopaedias or dictionaries. If the encyclopaedic works are more general, they should be organized under a separate general heading in alphabetical order according to the titles of the works.

Example:

Gran Enciclopedia Rialp. Madrid: Rialp, 1971–1977. 24 volumes.

New Catholic Encyclopaedia. New York: McGraw Hill, 1967. 12 volumes.

****

D. Books:
The works should be organized in alphabetical order, according to author. Two books by the same author are put in chronological order starting with the oldest. It is sufficient and preferable to give only initials for authors' Christian names. If a work is a translation, the name of the translator should be indicated, but the book should be placed alphabetically under the name of the original author.

Example:

AA.VV. *Science and the Modern World (Plenary Session held in March 1976) Part I.* Pontificiae Academiae Scientiarum Scripta Varia 42. Vatican City: Pontificia Academia Scientiarum, 1976.

——. *Scienza e non-credenza.* Vatican City: Segretariato per i non-credenti, 1980.

——. *Science and the Modern World (Plenary Session held in October 1978) Part II.* Pontificiae Academiae Scientiarum Scripta Varia 49. Vatican City: Pontificia Academia Scientiarum, 1983.

——. *Science and the Modern World (Plenary Session held in November 1979) Part III.* Pontificiae Academiae Scientiarum Scripta Varia 52. Vatican City: Pontificia Academia Scientiarum, 1984.

——. *Scienza e Sapienza. Atti della Solenne Commemorazione del primo centenario della morte di G. Gregor Mendel.* Roma: I Rilievi, 1984.

——. *Galileo Galilei: 350 anni di storia. Studi e ricerche.* Roma: Marietti, 1984.

Abrecht, P. (ed.). *Faith and Science in an Unjust World.* Vol. 2, 'Reports and Recommendations.' Philadelphia, Pa.: Fortress Press, 1980.

Austin, W. H. *The Relevance of Natural Science to Theology.* London: Macmillan, 1976.

von Balthasar, H. U. *Man in History: A Theological Study.* London: Sheed and Ward, 1968.

Barbour, I. G. *Issues in Science and Religion.* New York: Harper and Row, 1971.

Barrow, J. D., and Silk, J. *The Left Hand of Creation: the Origin and Evolution of the Expanding Universe.* New York: Basic Books, 1983.

Lambert, J. H. — *Cosmological Letters on the Arrangement of the World-Edifice*. Translated from German, with an Introduction and notes by S. L. Jaki. New York: Science History Publications, 1976.

E. Articles

The articles should be organized in alphabetical order, according to author. Two articles by the same author are put in chronological order starting with the oldest. For an article from a book or an encyclopaedia, 'In' is used to denote the source.

Example:

Caldecott, S.	'Cosmology, eschatology, ecology: Some reflections on *Sollicitudo Rei Socialis*.' *Communio* 15/3 (Fall 1988) pp.305–318.
Hodgson, P. E.	'A Duty to Share Knowledge.' *The Times* (27 April 1985) p.10.
Kasper, W.	'Hope in the final coming of Jesus Christ in Glory.' *Communio* 12/4 (Winter 1985) pp.368–384.
McDermott, J. M.	'Catholic Doctrine on Death.' In: R.J. White, H. Angstwurm and I. Carrasco de Paula (eds.), *The Determination of Brain Death and its Relationship with Human Death* (Città del Vaticano: Pontificia Academia Scientiarum, 1992) pp.153–176.
Ratzinger, J.	'Jesus Christ today.' *Communio* (Notre Dame) 17/1 (Spring 1990) pp.68-87.
Wilhelmsen, F. D.	'Realism.' In *New Catholic Encyclopaedia* (New York: McGraw Hill, 1967) Volume 12, pp.110–111.

****

F. Book Reviews:

These are arranged in alphabetical order of the name of the reviewer. If a reviewer is mentioned more than once, his or her reviews are placed in chronological order.

Example:

Jaki, S. L.	Review of L. Bouyer, *Cosmos et la gloire de Dieu* (Paris: Cerf, 1982) in *The Downside Review* 102 (1984) pp.301–307.
Juric, S.,	Review of S. L. Jaki, *Genesis 1 through the Ages* (London: Thomas More Press, 1992) in *Angelicum* 70/3 (1993) pp.450–451.

G. Archive Material

The material is arranged in chronological order, starting with the oldest.

Example:

Letter of Cardinal John Smith to Bishop Fred Jones, 28 September 1979. Archives of the Pontifical Council for General Welfare, Protocol N° 679/79; Position 401.

Letter of Sir John Jones to Mr. Alfred Johnstone, Chairman of the Department of Transport, Archives of the Department of Transport, Document N° 51643 of 1986.

H. Interviews

The material is arranged in chronological order, starting with the oldest

Example:

Interview with Rt. Rev. Adam Hayforth, Bishop of Appleford, 25th May 1989.

Interview with Mr. Jon Yu, 27th April 1994.

I. Anonymous Works

The first important word in the title determines alphabetical order. Should two anonymous works have the same first word, then they are classified according to the next important word in their title.

Example:

Anon., *A Day in the Life of a Theology Student*. Rome: Newtext, 1993.

Anon., *A Day without Sunset*. London: Smallbooks, 1932.